SPOTTER'S GUIDE TO
BUGS AND INSECTS

Anthony Wootton

Illustrated by Phil Weare

TED SMART

Edited by Philippa Wingate, Jessica Datta and Sue Jacquemier
Series editor: Philippa Wingate
Designed by Lucy Owen
Cover and series designer: Laura Fearn
Expert consultant: Margaret Rostron

Additional illustrations: Joyce Bee, Kuo Kang Chen, Ian Jackson
and Aziz Khan

Cover - Corbis/Ralph A.Clevinger; p.1 - Digital Vision; p.2-3 - © Dennis
Johnson: Papilio/Corbis; p.6-7 - © Robert Pickett/Corbis; p.9 - Ralph A.
Clevenger/Corbis; photographic backgrounds p.4-5, 8-64 Digital Vision.

First published in 2000 by Usborne Publishing Ltd., Usborne House,
83-85 Saffron Hill, London EC1N 8RT, England. www.usborne.com
Copyright © 2000, 1986, 1979 Usborne Publishing Ltd. The name
Usborne and the device ⊕ are Trade Marks of Usborne Publishing Ltd.

This edition produced for: The Book People Ltd, Hall Wood Avenue,
Haydock, St Helens, WA11 9UL

Printed in Spain

The caterpillar of an
Emperor Moth

CONTENTS

HOW TO USE THIS BOOK

This book is an identification guide to the insects of Britain and Europe. There are over 20,000 "species" or kinds of insect in Britain alone. This book includes a selection of them.

INSECT DESCRIPTIONS
Each insect in this book has a picture and a description next to it like the one below. The description tells you where the insect lives, where it lays its eggs and what it eats.

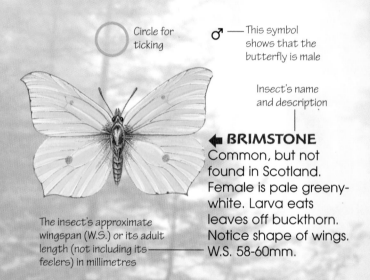

Circle for ticking

♂ — This symbol shows that the butterfly is male

Insect's name and description

◄ BRIMSTONE
Common, but not found in Scotland. Female is pale greeny-white. Larva eats leaves off buckthorn. Notice shape of wings. W.S. 58-60mm.

The insect's approximate wingspan (W.S.) or its adult length (not including its feelers) in millimetres

KEEPING SCORE
A scorecard on pages 59-62 gives you a score for each insect you spot. A common one scores 5 points, and a very rare one is worth 25.

DIFFICULT WORDS
Some of the more difficult words included in the descriptions in this book are explained in a glossary on pages 56 and 57.

MALE AND FEMALE

The males and females of some species differ from each other. In these cases, both males and females are usually shown. The symbol ♂ means male and ♀ means female.

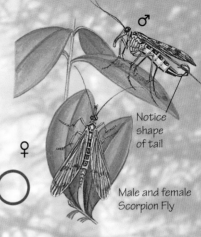

♂

♀

Notice shape of tail

Male and female Scorpion Fly

Adult Nut Weevil

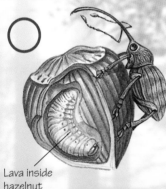

Lava inside hazelnut

If the young of an insect, known as its larva, is seen more often than the adult insect, or if it is particularly interesting, it is shown too. For example, this picture shows a Nut Weevil's larva living inside a hazelnut.

The British Isles

Scandinavia

Mainland Europe

AREAS COVERED

The green areas on this map show the countries covered by this book. Some insects may be very rare in the British Isles, but keep an eye out for them when you visit other European countries.

INTRODUCING INSECTS

This book is all about insects. Bugs are just one kind of insect. As you will see, different kinds of insect look very different from each other. However, all adult insects have six legs and their bodies have three distinct parts – a head, a thorax and an abdomen.

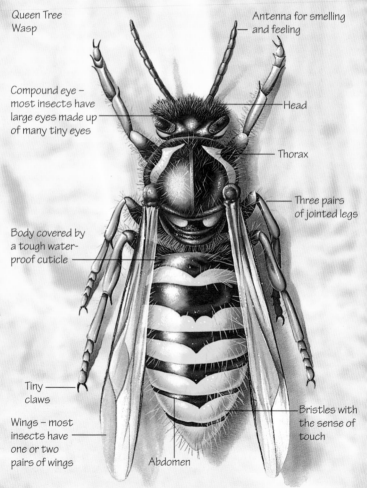

Queen Tree Wasp

Antenna for smelling and feeling

Compound eye – most insects have large eyes made up of many tiny eyes

Head

Thorax

Three pairs of jointed legs

Body covered by a tough water-proof cuticle

Tiny claws

Wings – most insects have one or two pairs of wings

Abdomen

Bristles with the sense of touch

AN INSECT'S LIFE-CYCLE

Most insects hatch from eggs. After hatching, they go through different stages of growth before becoming adults.

The eggs of some insects, such as butterflies and beetles, pass through two more stages before becoming adults – a larva stage and a pupa stage.

Some insects, such as bugs and dragonflies, lay eggs that hatch into larvae called nymphs. Nymphs look like small adults. They shed their skin several times, each time growing bigger. This is called moulting. A nymph's wings start as tiny buds, which grow bigger each time it moults.

These three pictures show a larva developing into a Swallowtail butterfly

This Grasshopper nymph looks very like an adult Grasshopper, but it does not have wings

1. The egg hatches into a larva known as a caterpillar

2. The caterpillar becomes a pupa. Inside, the pupa, the body of the caterpillar breaks down and becomes the body of the butterfly

3. The pupa splits and an adult emerges

LOOKING AT INSECTS

Insects can be found all year round, but summer is the best time to look. Wherever you live, you should be able to find a wide variety of species. These pages give you some tips about how to become a good insect spotter.

WHERE TO LOOK

A good place to spot a wide variety of bugs and insects is in an open green space, such as a field, a garden or a park. Look on flowers and leaves, in grass and soil, under stones, on tree bark, in water, and even inside houses.

You are most likely to spot Seven-spot Ladybirds on sunny days

KEEP YOUR EYES OPEN

Most insects are very small. Many fly or run fast and are coloured like the plants they live on. To be a successful insect spotter you must train your eyes to look closely at the places where insects live.

Concentrate on a small area at a time. Kneel or lie flat and look up at the undersides of leaves where insect may be hidden from the eyes of birds and other predators.

FOOD PLANTS

Some insects feed on only one kind of plant. this is called their "food plant". These plants will help you to identify an insect. The descriptions in this book contain information about a species' food plant.

WHAT TO TAKE SPOTTING

• take this book out spotting with you;
• a notebook and pencil to draw pictures of the insects you find and make notes about when and where you see them;
• a magnifying glass.

Found 6.7.00 on the bark of an oak tree yellow feelers and face. six legs

---

TAKE CARE
Remember, insects are very fragile. Don't pick them up or touch their wings.

FOOD AND FEEDING

Insects feed on all kinds of animals and plants. Insects are carnivores (meat-eaters), herbivores (plant-eaters) or omnivores (meat- and plant-eaters). Some insects, known as parasites, actually live on or inside the bodies of other living animals.

House-flies have suction pads at the end of their proboscises. Saliva passes into the pad and partly digests food before it is sucked into the fly's mouth.

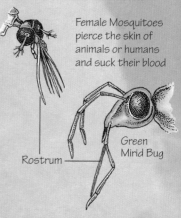

House-fly

Sucking pad

INSECT MOUTHPARTS

Insects use their mouthparts to suck up liquids, or to bite and chew solid food. Insects that suck have a hollow tube called a proboscis. Bees, butterflies and moths use a proboscis to suck nectar from flowers.

Some insects pierce plants and animals with a pointed tube called a rostrum.

Female Mosquitoes pierce the skin of animals or humans and suck their blood

Green Mirid Bug

Rostrum

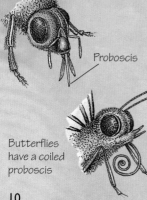

Bee

Proboscis

Butterflies have a coiled proboscis

Insects, such as beetles, that bite and chew have strong jaws.

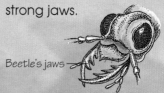

Beetle's jaws

10

SELF-DEFENCE

All insects are in constant danger of being eaten by other animals. Here are some of ways they defend themselves.

SHOCK TACTICS
Some insects sting, bite, or produce nasty smells or poisons to shock their enemies and give them time to escape. Other insects try to look dangerous, or make sudden movements to frighten their enemies.

A Bombardier Beetle fires a puff of poisonous gas at its enemies

COLOUR WARNING
Insects that taste unpleasant are often brightly coloured so that predators will avoid eating them. Some harmless insects protect themselves by copying the colours of bad-tasting or poisonous insects.

CAMOUFLAGE
The colour of many insects makes them difficult for predators to spot.

The Poplar Hawk Moth caterpillar is well disguised by colours and markings which match the leaves it feeds on

Shape can also be a camouflage. For example, stick insects and some caterpillars resemble twigs. Other insects can look like leaves, grass or seeds.

Stick insects look so like twigs they are hard to detect

BUTTERFLIES

Butterflies fly around during the day, unlike moths which are active at night.

➡ WALL BROWN
Found in dry, open places, on sunny walls and paths. Produce larvae twice a year (May-June and Aug.). Larva eats various grasses. W.S. 44-46mm.

⬅ MARBLED WHITE
Common on chalk in the south, but scarce elsewhere in England. Found on dry grassy banks and disused railways. Lays eggs on grasses. W.S. 53-58mm.

➡ PEARL-BORDERED FRITILLARY
Likes dog rose and wood violet flowers in woodland clearings. Lays eggs on violet. Found all over Britain, but most common in south. W.S. 42-46mm.

♀

Male's wings
have less black

⬅ HOLLY BLUE
Open woodland and gardens with tall holly trees. Larva eats flower buds of holly and ivy. Most common in south and east England. W.S. 33-35mm.

➤ PURPLE HAIRSTREAK

Flies round tops of oak trees. Like all Hairstreaks, larva is slug-like, but not slimy. Brownish larva eats oak leaves. W.S. 36-39 mm.

Male has more purplish blue on the wings

♀

◄ CLOUDED YELLOW

Sometimes arrives in spring from south Europe. Breeds here and lays eggs on clover and lucerne, but larvae do not survive our winters. W.S. 58-62mm.

➤ PEACOCK

Seen in gardens in spring and summer. Adults hibernate in winter, often in houses. Bristly black larva has tiny white spots, and eats nettles. W.S. 62-68mm.

♂

◄ BRIMSTONE

Common, but not found in Scotland. Female is pale greeny-white. Larva eats leaves off buckthorn. Notice shape of wings. W.S. 58-60mm.

13

MOTHS

Most moths are nocturnal, which means they are active at night. Moths' antennae don't have swellings at the ends like those of butterflies.

▶ DEATH'S-HEAD HAWK
Occasionally visits Britain from S. Europe and N. Africa. Lays eggs on potato leaves. Larva is seen in late summer and pupates underground. W.S. 100-125mm.

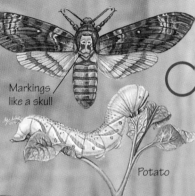

Markings like a skull

Potato

Privet

◀ PRIVET HAWK
Most common in southern England and midlands. Larva eats privet leaves in July and August. Moth emerges the following summer. W.S. 90-100mm.

▶ LIME HAWK
One of Britain's most common hawk moths. Larva eats leaves of lime trees in late summer. W.S. 65-70mm.

Lime

➡ EYED HAWK

Flashes markings on its underwings to frighten birds and other enemies. Larva feeds on sallow and leaves of plum and apple trees. W.S. 75-80mm.

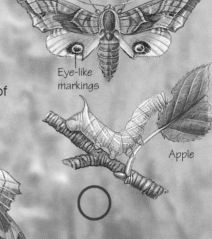

Eye-like markings

Apple

Yellow points

⬅ POPLAR HAWK

Common all over Britain. Larva feeds on poplar or willow and, like Eyed Hawk, has rough skin surface. Notice yellow markings. W.S. 75-80mm.

Poplar

➡ HUMMINGBIRD HAWK

Visitor to Britain. Found in gardens during day. Hovers over flowers to feed, beating its wings like a hummingbird. Lays eggs on bedstraw plants. W.S. 45mm.

Bedstraw

15

MOTHS

➡ ELEPHANT HAWK
Widespread, but scarce in Scotland. Larva is shaped like an elephant's trunk. It feeds on willowherb and bedstraw plant. W.S. 65mm.

Willowherb

♀

♂

Sloe

◀ EMPEROR
Found all over Britain. Male flies by day over moorland, looking for female which comes out at dusk. Lays eggs on heather and brambles. Appearance of larva changes each time its skin is shed. W.S. female 70mm. Male 55mm.

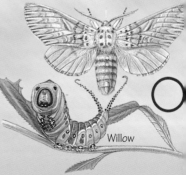

➡ PUSS
Widespread in Britain. Lays eggs, usually singly, on willow in May-June. Thin red "whips" come out of larva's tails, perhaps to frighten birds. W.S. 65-80mm.

Willow

➡ LOBSTER
Can be seen in southern
England, Wales and
parts of southern Ireland.
Name comes from the
shape of the larva's tail
end. Larva eats beech
leaves. W.S. 65-70mm.

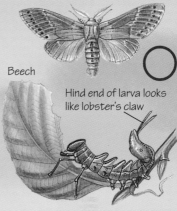

Beech

Hind end of larva looks
like lobster's claw

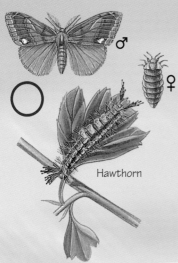

♂

♀

Hawthorn

◀ VAPOURER
Common all over Britain,
even in towns. Female
has only wing stubs and
can't fly. Larva feeds
on a variety of trees.
W.S. 35mm.

Peach blossom pattern

Bramble

➡ PEACH BLOSSOM
Found in woodland
areas. Its name comes
from the peach blossom
pattern on its wings.
Larva feeds on bramble.
W.S. 35mm.

MOTHS

← YELLOW-TAIL
Brightly coloured larvae are often found in hedgerows of hawthorn, sloe and bramble in May and June. W.S. 32-40mm.

Hawthorn

Merveille-du-Jour

→ MERVEILLE-DU-JOUR
Lives in oak woodlands. Forewings match oak tree bark, making moth difficult for enemies to see. Larva eats oak leaves. W.S. 45mm.

Oak

Alder Moth

Alder

← ALDER
Like many other species, the larva is more striking than the adult moth. It feeds on a variety of trees, including alder and oak. W.S. 37mm.

➡ CLIFDEN NONPAREIL or BLUE UNDERWING

Breeds in a few places in Kent, but sometimes visits other parts of Britain, usually in late summer. Stick-like larva feeds on black poplar and aspen.

Colour of upper wings matches tree bark

Larva of Red Underwing

Willow

⬅ RED UNDERWING

Quite common in southern England and midlands. Flashes underwings when threatened by birds. Rests in daytime on trees. Larva eats poplar and willow. W.S. 80mm.

➡ MOTHER SHIPTON

Flies on sunny days. Look on railway banks and in meadows May to June. Larva eats vetches and clover. Named after a woman who was believed to be able to see into the future. W.S. 35mm.

Face-like marking on wings

Clover

Lava of Mother Shipton

19

MOTHS

Y-shaped markings

◀ SILVER Y
Visitor to Britain, some years in great numbers. Feeds on garden flowers with long proboscis. Flies fast. Larva eats nettle and thistle. W.S. 40mm.

➡ HERALD
Widespread in Britain. Hibernates during the winter in barns, sometimes in small groups. Mates in spring and female lays eggs on various kinds of willow. W.S. 40mm.

Larva of Herald

Willow

♂

◀ OAK EGGAR
Male flies by day searching for female who rests in heather on moorland. Larva eats heather, bramble and hawthorn. W.S. 50-65mm.

Female is larger and paler

Hawthorn

20

➡ LAPPET

Name comes from "lappets" on larva. Feeds on apple, willow and hawthorn. Adult's brown colour, ragged wing edges and veined wings make it look like a bunch of leaves. W.S. 60-70mm.

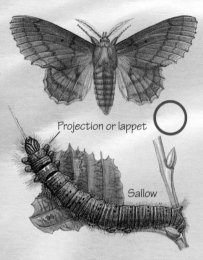

Projection or lappet

Sallow

Wing pattern varies

⬅ WOOD TIGER

Smaller and more local than Garden Tiger. Widespread on hillsides, heaths and open woodland. Larva eats violets and forget-me-nots and hibernates. W.S. 35-40 mm.

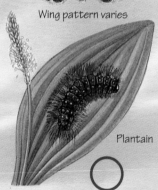

Plantain

➡ GARDEN TIGER

Common, but larva more often seen. Feeds on many low-growing plants and hibernates when young. Feeds again in spring and is fully grown by June. W.S. 60-70mm.

Larva is called a woolly bear

21

MOTHS

➡ CINNABAR
Sometimes flies by
day but weakly. Striped
larvae feed in groups
on ragwort. Common
on waste ground
and railway banks.
W.S. 40-45mm.

Ragwort

Larva inside
tree trunk

⬅ GOAT
Widespread, but well
camouflaged and rarely
seen. Larva eats wood of
ash and willow. Spends
three or four years in a
tree trunk and pupates
a silk-bonded cocoon
made of wood shavings.
Larva smells like goats.
W.S. 70-85mm.

➡ SWALLOW-TAILED
Looks like a butterfly.
Weak, fluttering flight.
Stick-like larva feeds on
leaves of ivy, hawthorn
and sloe. W.S. 56mm.

← SIX-SPOT BURNET
The most common British burnet. Flies over grassy areas during the day. Larva eats trefoil, clover and vetch. Boat-shaped cocoons are found attached to plant stems. W.S. 35mm.

→ GHOST
Very common. Males often seen after dusk searching for larger females in dense grass. Female clings without moving to grass stem until male approaches. Larva eats plant roots. W.S. 50-60mm.

Female is better camouflaged than male

← FORESTER
Widely distributed. Flies over lush meadows. Stubby larva feeds on sorrel. W.S. 25-27mm.

BEETLES

➡ GREEN TIGER BEETLE

Fierce, sharp-jawed predator. Open woodland and sandy areas in early summer. Larva catches ants when they approach its burrow. 12-15 mm long.

Larva in burrow

Most beetles have a pair of hard wing cases called elytra

⬅ LARGE GREEN GROUND BEETLE

Adults live in oak trees. Both adults and larvae feed on leaf-eating caterpillars and other larvae. 16-20mm long.

➡ VIOLET GROUND BEETLE

Found under large stones in gardens, and common in woods and under hedges. Adult and larva eat other insects and worms. Larva pupates in soil. 30-35mm long.

Gas from abdomen

⬅ BOMBARDIER BEETLE

Lives under stones in chalky areas in southern England. When threatened, it shoots irritating gas from end of its abdomen with a popping sound. 7-10mm long.

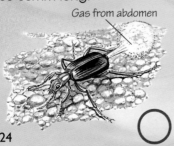

Larva

➡ ROVE BEETLE
Feeds mainly on dead animals and birds. Most common in southern England. Related to Devil's Coach Horse. 20mm long.

Mouse

➡ ANT BEETLE
Small, fast-moving beetle found on elms and conifers. Larvae live under loose bark. Adults and larvae eat larvae of bark beetles. 7-10mm long.

⬅ DEVIL'S COACH HORSE or COCKTAIL BEETLE
Common in gardens. When challenged, raises tail and spreads jaws. Can ooze poisonous liquid from end of abdomen. 25-30mm long.

⬅ RED AND BLACK BURYING BEETLE
Feeds on dead animals, kneading and biting the flesh and then burying the body. Female lays eggs in burrow beside the body. Larvae feed on it and pupate in a chamber in soil. 15-20mm long.

25

BEETLES

➡ GREAT DIVING BEETLE

Lives in lakes and large ponds. Eats tadpoles, small fish and other insects. Collects air from surface and stores it between wing covers and end of abdomen. 30-35mm long.

Male's wing cases are smoother than female's

♀

Larva

Carries bubble of air under body

◀ GREAT SLIVER WATER BEETLE

Largest British water beetle. Eats mainly water plants, but larva is a predator and eats water snails. Can fly to other waters if its home dries up. 37-48mm long.

➡ WHIRLIGIG BEETLE

Seen in groups on surface of ponds, lakes and slow rivers in bright sunshine. Darts in all directions. Carnivorous, eating mosquito larvae. 6-8mm long.

◀ WATER BEETLE

Lives under water, among vegetation of lakes and rivers, where it lays its eggs. Colour may be darker, sometimes all black. Widespread. 7-8mm long.

➡ GLOW-WORM

Likes grassy banks, hillsides, open woods. Most common in S. England. Wingless female attracts male with her glowing tail. ♂ Male 15mm long. Female 20mm long.

Larva

⬅ LESSER GLOW-WORM

Seen near streams on damp grassy banks. Male and larva have small lights on tip of abdomen. Found in central and southern Europe, but not in Britain. 8-10mm long.

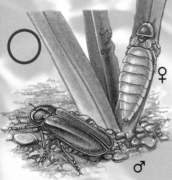

♀

♂

➡ SCARLET-TIPPED FLOWER BEETLE

Most common in southern England. Look in buttercups and other flowerheads. Blows up scarlet bladders on its underside when handled. 7-10mm long.

Buttercup

⬅ CLICK BEETLE or SKIPJACK

Found in dense vegetation or in flowers. Larvae live in soil, eating plant roots. Other species of Click Beetle do much damage to crops. 14-18mm long.

Larva is called a wireworm

27

BEETLES

➡ TWO-SPOT LADYBIRD

Very common. Colour pattern often varies and some individuals are shiny black with red spots. 4-5mm long.

Ladybird eating aphid

Rose

⬅ SEVEN-SPOT LADYBIRD

Very common. Hibernates in large numbers in sheds, houses or tree bark. Emerges on sunny spring days to find aphids and lay its eggs. 6-7mm long.

➡ EYED LADYBIRD

Largest ladybird in Britain. Found near or on fir trees. Both adults and larvae hunt for aphids. 8-9mm long.

22-spot Ladybird   14-spot Ladybird

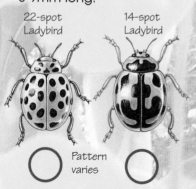

Pattern varies

⬅ 22-SPOT LADYBIRD
⬅ 14-SPOT LADYBIRD

22-spot is found in many areas and habitats. 2-3mm long. 14-spot is rare in the north. Likes trees and bushes. 3-4mm long.

➡ DEATHWATCH BEETLE

Larva eats timber in buildings. The sound the adult makes when it taps its head against its tunnel walls was once believed to fortell a death. 7-10mm long.

⬅ CARDINAL BEETLE

Found on flowers and under bark. Whitish larvae feed on bark and wood. 15-17mm long.

➡ OIL BEETLE

This beetle cannot fly. The larva waits in a flower for a special kind of solitary bee to carry it to its nest where the larva feeds and grows. 15-30mm long.

⬅ BLISTER BEETLE

Rare. Name comes from a fluid in the insect's blood which causes blisters on human skin. Larvae live as parasites in the nests of some types of bee. 12-20mm long.

BEETLES

➡ STAG BEETLE

Largest British beetle.
Only male has antlers.
Larvae feed on tree
stumps for three years
or more. Most common
in the southern
England. 25-27mm long.

Antlers

♂

⬅ DOR BEETLE

Common. Seen flying at
night to dung heaps
where it lays its eggs.
Makes a loud droning
sound when it flies.
16-24mm long.

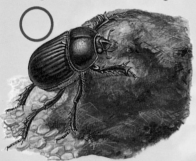

➡ HORNED DUNG BEETLE or MINOTAUR BEETLE

Found in sandy places
where rabbits live. Eats
their dung and fills tunnels
with it for larvae to eat.
12-18mm long.

⬅ COCKCHAFER or MAY BUG

Common. Flies round tree
tops in early summer and
sometimes down chimneys
and at lighted windows.
Larvae may be dug up in
gardens. 25-30mm long.

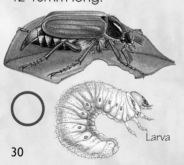

Larva

➡ ROSE CHAFER
Sometimes found in roses and other flowers. Larvae feed on old timber and roots. Found all over Britain. 14-20mm long.

Rose

⬅ BEE BEETLE
Found mainly in Scotland and Wales. Found in flowers. Mimics colouring of bees (see page 11). Larvae eat rotting wood. 10-13mm long.

➡ MUSK BEETLE
Longhorn beetles have long antennae, perhaps so they can recognize each other when they emerge from their pupae in wood tunnels. 20-32mm long.

Long "horns"

Willow

⬅ WASP BEETLE
Harmless, but looks and behaves like a wasp. Flies in bright sunshine visiting flowers. Common throughout Britain. 15mm long.

31

BEETLES

➡ COLORADO BEETLE
Damages potato crops.
Introduced by accident
from America. Some still
appear in Europe. You
should tell the police if you
spot one. 10-12mm long.

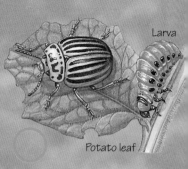

Larva

Potato leaf

⬅ BLOODY-NOSED BEETLE
Like Oil Beetle and Blister
Beetle, it reacts when
threatened, spurting bright
red fluid from its mouth. This
is called "reflex-bleeding".
Found in low dense foliage.
10-20mm long.

➡ GREEN TORTOISE BEETLE
Legs and antennae often
hidden so it looks like a
tortoise. Well camouflaged
on thistles where it feeds,
and where larvae pupate.
6-8mm long.

Larva has fork
in its tail

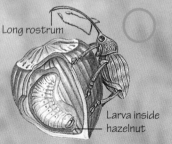

Long rostrum

Larva inside
hazelnut

⬅ NUT WEEVIL
Female uses her long
rostrum to pierce a young
hazelnut, where she lays
her single egg. Larva grows
inside the nut, eating the
kernel. 10mm long.

BUGS

➡ GREEN SHIELDBUG
Lives on trees such as hazel and birch. Lays eggs in batches. Nymphs mature in late summer after several moults. 12-14mm long.

Birch

White dead-nettle plant

⬅ PIED SHIELDBUG
Lays eggs in soil and female looks after them. When they hatch out, she leads the nymphs to their food plant. Rare in the north. 6-8mm long.

➡ HEATH ASSASSIN BUG
Common on open heath and sand dunes. Adults and nymphs suck body fluids out of prey. Most adults are wingless. 9-12mm long.

Oak

⬅ FOREST BUG
Common on oak or orchard trees. Feeds on leaves, fruits and caterpillars. Female lays batches of eggs on leaves. 11-14mm long.

33

BUGS

➡ WATER CRICKET

Common on still and slow-moving water. Runs on water surface, eating insects and spiders. Lays eggs out of water on moss. 6-7mm long.

Breathing tube

◀ WATER SCORPION

Found in ponds and shallow lakes. Seizes small fish tadpoles and insect larvae with its forelegs. Lays eggs in algae or on water plants. 18-22mm long.

➡ WATER STICK INSECT

Not related to true stick insects, but like them it is hard to see among plants. Most common in southern Wales and southern England. 30-35mm long.

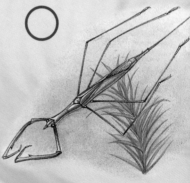

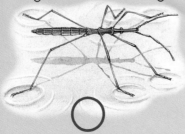

◀ WATER MEASURER

Found at edges of ponds and slow rivers and streams. Stabs at mosquito larvae and water fleas with its rostrum. Also eats dead insects. 9-12mm long.

➤ WATER BOATMAN
or BACKSWIMMER

Lives in pools, canals, ditches and water tanks. Jerks along with its hind legs, usually on its back. Eats tadpoles and small fish. Can fly away if its home dries up. 15mm long.

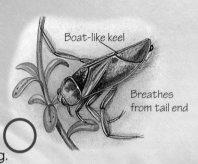

Boat-like keel

Breathes from tail end

◀ LESSER WATER
BOATMAN

Flatter and rounder than Water Boatman, with shorter legs. It uses its front legs to swim. Sucks up bits of animal and plant material at bottom of ponds. Common. 12-14mm long.

➤ POND SKATER

Front legs adapted to catch dead or dying insects that fall on water's surface. Some can fly; others have no wings. Common in ponds. 8-10mm long.

◀ SAUCER BUG

Lives in vegetation at bottom of muddy pools and canals. Like the Water Boatman, it can stab you with its rostrum. Hibernates in winter, as do most water bugs. 12-16mm long.

35

BUGS

➡ NEW FOREST CICADA

Male makes high-pitched buzzing sound that is very difficult to hear. Nymphs live underground for several years eating plant roots. The only British cicada. 25mm long.

Adult sucks sap from trees

Birch

○

⬅ SOUTHERN CICADA

Larger and noisier than British cicada. Common in southern Europe. Adult eats the sap of ash, pine and olive trees. 50mm long.

○   ○

➡ HORNED TREEHOPPER

Found on tree branches and low vegetation, such as bracken, in woods. Adult and larva feed on oak leaves and other plants. 9-10m long.

Bracken

⬅ BLACK AND RED FROGHOPPER

Common in dense grass and on trees. Jumps if disturbed. Larvae secrete froth which covers them when they feed under-ground. 9-10mm long.

○

➡ EARED LEAFHOPPER

Seen on lichen-covered oak or other trees where it is well hidden. Adults appear about June. Moves slowly. Local in southern England. 13-17mm long.

Ear-like projections

⬅ GREEN LEAFHOPPER

Common throughout Britain. Feeds on grasses and rushes in damp meadows and marshy places. 6-9mm long.

➡ ROSE APHID or GREENFLY

Green or pinkish. Feeds on roses in spring, then moves to other plants. Excretes honeydew which ants feed on. Pest on roses. 2-3mm long.

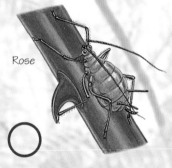

Rose

⬅ BEAN APHID or BLACKFLY

Common on broad bean, but also on thistle and other plants. Lays eggs on spindle trees. Adults produce fully-formed young which eat beans. 2-3mm long.

DRAGONFLIES AND DAMSELFLIES

➡ DOWNY EMERALD
This dragonfly flies fast
and hovers over ponds,
lakes and slow-moving
streams and rivers in
summer. Quite common
in southern England.
W.S. 68mm.

Female is
longer than
male

⬅ GOLDEN-RINGED DRAGONFLY
Lives near streams and
rivers, but like many
dragonflies, it is
sometimes seen far from
water. Female lays eggs
in mud. W.S. 100 mm.

➡ BROAD-BODIED LIBELLULA
Seen over ponds and
lakes with plenty of plants.
Flies in short bursts. Most
common in southern
England. W.S. 75mm.

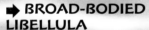

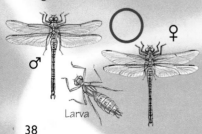

Larva

⬅ EMPEROR DRAGONFLY
Seen over large ponds,
lakes and canals in the
summer. Adult catches
flies in flight. W.S. 105mm.

➡ RUDDY DARTER

Found near weedy ponds or ditches in marshy areas. Nymphs mature more quickly than the larger dragonflies, which may take 2-3 years. W.S. 55mm.

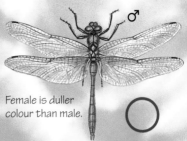

Female is duller colour than male.

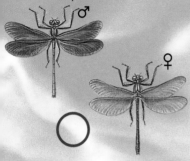

⬅ DEMOISELLE AGRION

Found near fast-flowing streams with sandy or stony bottoms. Damselflies usually rest with wings together, not spread out like dragonflies. W.S. 58-63mm.

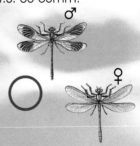

➡ BANDED AGRION

More common than the Demoiselle, but rare in northern England and not recorded in Scotland. Usually seen by streams and rivers with muddy bottoms. W.S. 60-65mm.

⬅ COMMON ISCHNURA or BLUE-TAILED DAMSELFLY

Found on plants by ditches, canals, lakes, ponds and slow-moving rivers and streams. Common in most of Britain. W.S. 35mm.

39

BEES, WASPS AND ANTS

Some bees, wasps and ants are solitary creatures. Others are "social insects", living in colonies. These colonies include queens, drones and workers.

➡ RED-TAILED BUMBLEBEE
Common in gardens. The queen makes a nest in a hole in the ground. Eggs develop into colonies of queens, workers and drones. Queen 22mm long.

Nest

Leaves cut by bee

⬅ LEAF-CUTTER BEE
Cuts pieces from rose leaves to make cylinders where female lays an egg. Solitary species. Male 10mm long. Female 11mm.

➡ POTTER WASP
Makes clay pots for its larvae. Each one has a separate pot, stocked with smaller caterpillars (paralyzed with a sting) for food. Sandy heaths. Male 12mm long. Female 14mm.

Pot

⬅ SAND WASP
Makes a nest burrow in sand where it lays a single egg on top of a paralyzed caterpillar. Larva eats the caterpillar. 28-30mm long.

➡ RUBY-TAILED WASP

Also called a cuckoo-wasp because female lays egg in nest of a solitary bee or wasp. When larva hatches it eats its host's food and its egg or larva. 12mm long.

♀

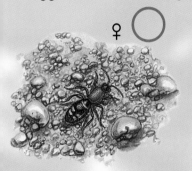

⬅ VELVET ANT

Actually a wasp, but female is wingless. She lays her egg in a bee larva which is eaten by her own larva when it hatches. Can sting painfully. 15mm long.

Female is larger than male

♀

Ovipositor is 35mm long

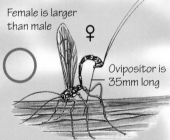

➡ ICHNEUMON WASP

Female pierces pine trees with her ovipositor (egg layer) and lays an egg on a Horntail larva or in its burrow inside the tree. 22-30mm long.

♂

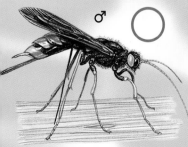

⬅ GIANT WOOD WASP or HORNTAIL

Female lays eggs in sickly or felled conifers. Larvae feed on wood for up to three years. 25-32mm long.

WASPS

➡ BLUE HORNTAIL
Male is like male Horntail except his head, thorax and the first two segments of his abdomen are deep metallic blue. Female is all blue and has only a short ovipositor. 20-25mm long.

Ovipositor

Dog rose

⬅ HORNET
Not as likely to sting as the German Wasp. Nests in hollow trees, banks or roofs. Preys on soft-bodied insects with which it feeds its larvae. Also feeds from flowers in woods. 22-30mm long.

➡ GERMAN WASP
One of the most common British species. Most likely to sting in late summer when larvae are mature. 15-20mm long.

Marmalade

Wasp's nest in tree

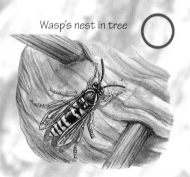

⬅ TREE WASP
Likes to nest in woods, often hanging its oval nest from a tree branch. More locally distributed than Common or German Wasps. 15-20mm long.

ANTS

➡ CARPENTER ANT
Hollows out pine tree trunks where it nests, often making the tree fall down. Not in Britain. 8-18mm long.

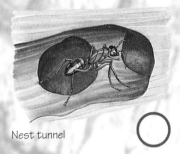

Nest tunnel

⬅ WOOD ANT
Makes large conical nest from twigs and leaves in pine woods. Useful to foresters as it eats leaf-eating larvae. Cannot sting, but sprays formic acid at intruders. 5-11mm long.

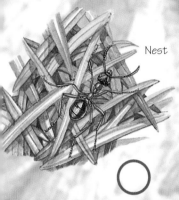

Nest

➡ RED ANT
Nests under stones or in rotting wood. Rears aphids in its nest and feeds on the sugary liquid they produce. 3-6mm long.

Nest in tree stump

⬅ BLACK ANT
Common in gardens. Like all ants, only queens and males have wings. Males die after mating and queens start a new colony. 3-9mm long.

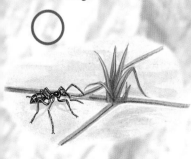

ANT, SAWFLY, GALL-WASPS

➡ YELLOW MEADOW ANT

Makes small mounds in meadows. Sometimes "farms" other small insects, such as aphids, for a sugary liquid that they produce. 2-9mm long.

⬅ BIRCH SAWFLY

Name "sawfly" comes from female's saw-like ovipositor. Larva feeds on birch leaves in late summer. It makes a large oval cocoon and the adult emerges the next spring. 20-23mm long.

Sawfly larva has nine pairs of legs

➡ OAK MARBLE GALL-WASP

Female lays egg in a leaf bud. Larva's feeding causes the tree to "blister" around it. Only one larva lives in each "marble". 4mm long.

Marble gall

⬅ OAK APPLE GALL-WASP

These galls can be 40mm across and are at first red and green and then later darken. Each gall contains many larvae. Insect is 3mm long.

Oak apple gall

44

TRUE FLIES

True flies have only one pair of wings. The second pair are replaced by two "halteres", which are like tiny drumsticks. Flies probably use them for balance. The insects that appear on pages 48-50 are not true flies.

➡ GREY FLESH FLY
Common. Lays eggs in carrion. White, legless larvae (known as maggots) feed on flesh before turning into oval brown pupae. 6-17mm.

Rat

⬅ GREENBOTTLE FLY
Most species lay eggs in carrion. Adults seen on flowers. One species lays eggs in skin or fleece of sheep. Its larvae eat the sheep's flesh. 7-11mm long.

➡ DRONE FLY
Makes a loud, bee-like droning in flight. Visits flowers for nectar and pollen. Larva rests on the pond bottom and breathes through a long tube. 15mm long.

Breathing tube

⬅ HOVER FLY
Hovers as though motionless. Common in summer. Female lays eggs among aphids and the legless larvae eat them. 10-14mm long.

Antirrhinum flower

45

TRUE FLIES

➡ DUNG FLY

Visits fresh cowpats where female lays eggs. Rise in a buzzing mass if disturbed, but soon settle again. Larvae eat dung but adults are predators on other flies. 10-12mm long.

Cow pat

Robber Fly killing Damsel Fly

⬅ ROBBER FLY

Preys on other insects by capturing them and sucking out their body fluids. Larvae feed on animal dung as well as vegetable matter. 18-26mm long.

➡ BEE FLY

Probes flowers in gardens for nectar in spring. Lays eggs near bees' nests and its larvae eat the bees' larvae. Most common in S. England. 10-11mm long.

Sweet woodruff

⬅ HORSE FLY

Female sucks blood, but her loud hum warns you before you get bitten. Smaller species are more silent and stab before being noticed. Found in old forests in S. England. 20-25mm long.

A Horse Fly piercing someone's arm

➡ FEVER FLY

Does not bite or cause fever. Most noticeable in spring and summer. Males perform courtship dance in the air above females. 8mm long.

Water violet

⬅ GIANT CRANEFLY or DADDY-LONG-LEGS

Often found near water. Other species found in gardens where larvae (called leatherjackets) eat root crops and grass roots. 30-40mm long.

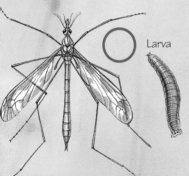

Larva

➡ BLACK AND YELLOW CRANEFLY

Found in low vegetation. Craneflies mate end to end and can be seen joined like this in summer. Female lays eggs in soil with her pointed ovipositor. 18-20mm long.

⬅ COMMON GNAT or MOSQUITO

Female sucks people's blood. Lays eggs in clusters which float on water. Larvae hang down below surface. 6-7mm long.

Water surface

47

ANT-LION, LACEWINGS

➡ ANT-LION
Name refers to larva which traps ants and other insects in a sandy hollow. Grabs them in its sickle-like jaws and sucks them dry. Not in Britain. Adult 35mm long.

Larva in hollow

⬅ GIANT LACEWING
Mainly nocturnal. Larvae eat small midge larvae they find in wet moss at water's edge. Pupate in silken yellowish cocoons. 15mm long.

➡ GREEN LACEWING
Found in gardens and hedges and sometimes attracted to house lights. Weak fluttering flight. Larvae feed on aphids. 15mm long.

Larva catching an aphid

⬅ BROWN LACEWING
Smaller than Green Lacewing, with dark brownish transparent wings. Look near water in lush vegetation and on trees. Throughout Britain. 10mm long.

SCORPION FLY, ALDER FLY, SNAKE FLY

➡ SCORPION FLY

Name comes from the scorpion-like shape of male's tail. Both adults and larvae eat dead insects and waste matter. 18-22mm long.

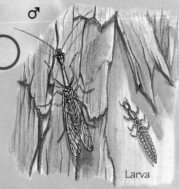

♂

♀

Notice shape of tail

◀ ALDER FLY

Slow, heavy flier. Lays eggs on stems of water plants. Larvae live on water bottom where they eat small animals. 20mm long.

Egg mat

➡ SNAKE FLY

Name comes from long head and thorax, which can bend, making the insect look like a cobra snake. 15-20mm long.

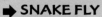

♂

Larva

CADDIS FLY, STONEFLY, MAYFLY

➡ CADDIS FLY
Found near lakes and slow rivers. Many caddis larvae make a protective case from bits of twigs and tiny shells. 15-20mm long.

Caddis larva in case made of leaves

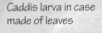

Wings overlap

⬅ STONEFLY
Found mainly in fast-flowing rivers. Larvae live at river bottom feeding on other small animals. 22mm long.

Larva on river bottom

Long tails

➡ MAYFLY
Adults live for a short time, perhaps only a few hours. In this time they mate and female lays her eggs in river water. 40mm long.

Long tails

CRICKETS

Crickets and bush crickets have very long antennae, while grasshoppers' are short. The third pair of legs on these insects is adapted for leaping. Males "sing" to attract females by rubbing their wing-cases together.

➡ FIELD CRICKET
Very rare. Lives in grassy banks and meadows in sandy or chalky areas. Male sings to attract female. 20mm long.

⬅ HOUSE CRICKET
Found in heated buildings and greenhouses, garden rubbish heaps and bigger tips. Rarely flies. Shrill song. 16mm long.

➡ MOLE CRICKET
Burrows like a mole with its large spade-like forefeet. Lives in damp meadows. Male has a whirring call. Rare. 38-42mm long.

⬅ WOOD CRICKET
Found in dead leaves in ditches and banks in southern England. Male has quiet churring song. Flightless. 8-9mm long.

GRASS HOPPER, BUSH CRICKETS

Wings look silvery in flight

◀ LARGE MARSH GRASSHOPPER
Found in bog and fenland in southern England, Norfolk Broads and Ireland. Flies a long way when disturbed. Male makes slow ticking sound. 27-32mm long.

▶ GREAT GREEN BUSH CRICKET
Harsh, shrill, penetrating song. Moves slowly and never flies far. Eats small insects found in dense vegetation. 45-47mm long.

Long hind legs

◀ SPECKLED BUSH CRICKET
Flightless adults seen in late summer or early autumn. Found in old gardens where shrubs grow. Male's song is hard to hear. 11-13mm long.

▶ WART-BITER
May bite when handled. Some people used to use it to bite their warts off. Seen in coarse grassland on downs. Preys on small insects. 34-35mm long.

COCKROACHES, MANTIS

➡ COMMON COCKROACH
Found in houses and other warm buildings, where it eats waste. Female lays eggs in purse-like containers. Does not fly. 25mm long.

Old bread

⬅ GERMAN COCKROACH
Not from Germany – it probably originated in N. Africa or the Middle East. Lives in heated buildings. 13mm long.

➡ DUSKY COCKROACH
Lives out-of-doors, unlike its larger relatives. Found mainly in woodlands on leaves of trees. 7-10mm long.

⬅ PRAYING MANTIS
Holds its forelegs together, as if praying, while waiting for its insect prey to come close. Found in scrub and tall grass in southern Europe. Not in Britain. 60-80mm long

STICK INSECT, EARWIGS

➡ STICK INSECT
Lives in bushes in
southern Europe.
Eats vegetation.
Another species is
commonly kept as a
pet. Not found in Britain.
Up to 90mm long.

⬅ COMMON EARWIG
Eats small insects (usually
dead), as well as leaves
and fruits. Female guards
nymphs until they can
look after themselves.
15mm long.

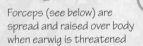

Forceps (see below) are
spread and raised over body
when earwig is threatened

➡ LESSER EARWIG
Flies during the day, but is
rarely noticed because it
is small. Not rare, but
less common than
Common Earwig.
10mm long.

SOME OTHER SMALL INSECTS

The insects on these pages are mostly very small and the pictures are greatly enlarged. The sizes given are very approximate.

← WATER SPRINGTAIL

Lives on the surface of ponds and lakes. Can make spectacular jumps by flicking its tail (usually folded beneath its body). About 2mm long.

→ FLEAS

Many different species. Wingless, but can jump powerfully. Feed on blood of many mammals and birds. Closely related to flies. Average length is 2mm.

← TERMITES

Like ants, termites are social insects with queens, soldiers and workers. Live in colonies in rotting wood. Not found in Britain. Average length is 10-15mm.

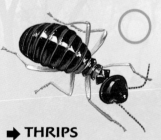

→ THRIPS

Tiny insects. Often settle on arms in hot summers and tickle. They are known as "thunder flies" because they are associated with thundery weather. About 1-2mm long.

USEFUL WORDS

This glossary explains some of the terms used in this book. The definitions refer specifically to insects, although some of the words can be used to refer to other animals. Words in *italic* text are defined separately in this glossary.

abdomen – the hind section of an insect.
algae – tiny water plants.
antenna (plural: antennae) – a pair of feelers on an insect's head used for feeling and smelling.

camouflage – when an insect's colour makes it difficult to see against certain backgrounds.
carnivores – insects that feed on other animals.
carrion – dead flesh. Some insects feed on the flesh of dead animals.
castes – different physical forms in *colonies* which have different functions.
chrysalis – see *pupa*.
cocoon – a case which protects an insect *pupa* made by the *larva* before it pupates.

colony – a group of insects that live together.
compound eye – eye made up of many lenses.

drone – male *social insect*.

entomology – the study of insects.
excrete – to get rid of waste from the body.

food plants – a plant that an insect species feeds on.

herbivores – insects that feed on plants.
hibernation – when an insect spends the winter in a sleepy state.
honeydew – a sweet liquid excreted by some insects.
host – an insect that is attacked by a *parasite*.

larva (plural: larvae) – The young stage of an insect which is very different from the adult insect.
local – insects that are found only in certain areas.

mandibles – the biting, piercing and cutting mouthparts of an insect.

metamorphosis – the process of changing from an egg to an adult, via a *larva* and (often) a *pupa*.

mimicry – when an insect's shape or colour copies that of another species, sometimes of a different order.

moult – the shedding of an insect's skin to allow growth.

nectar – a sweet–tasting liquid produced by flowers.

nocturnal – active at night.

nymph – A young miniature of the adult insect, which acquire wings during growth.

omnivores – insects that feed on plants and animals.

order – one of the scientific divisions of animals.

ovipositor – a female insect's egg-laying organ.

parasite – an insect that feeds off another animal's body without killing it.

predator – an insect that kills and eats other animals.

prey – an insect hunted by *predators*.

proboscis – the long, tube–like tongue of some insects.

pupa (plural: pupae) – the stage after the larval stage, during which the adult insect develops.

queen – a female *social insect* which lays eggs.

rostrum – the long, tube-like stabbing mouthpart of bugs and weevils.

scavenger – an insect that feeds on waste and dead matter.

secrete – when an insect's body produces and gives off a chemical from a gland.

social insects – insects that live in *colonies* and are organized so that each of the *castes* have different duties.

species – a group of insects that can breed together.

thorax – the middle section of an insect to which the legs and wings are attached.

worker – female *social insect* that cannot breed. These insects work for the *colony*.

CLUBS AND WEB SITES

Joining a club or society is a good way to find out more about insects and to meet other people who share your interest. Here are some organizations you can contact.

Entomological and Natural History Society

The Pelham-Clinton Building,
Dinton Pastures Country Park,
Davis Street,
Hurst, Reading,
Berkshire RG10 0TH

Amateur Entomologists' Society

PO Box 8774,
London, UK
SW7 5ZG
e-mail: aes@theaes.org

The Bug Club

(a club set up by the Amateur Entomologist Society for enthusiasts under 15years olds)
The Bug Club
AES
PO Box 8774,
London, UK
SW7 5ZG

You will find lots of information about insects on-line. Here are some Web sites to visit.

The Natural History Museum Discovering Entomology – entomology projects at the Natural History Museum.
http://www.nhm.ac.uk/science/entom/

Edinburgh Butterfly & Insect World – includes an on-line journey through a rainforest, scorpions, leaf cutter ants, and lots more.
http://www.edinburgh-butterfly-world.co.uk/

AES Bug Club – the Web site of a club for young entomology enthusiasts.
http://www.ex.ac.uk/bugclub/

The British Entomological and Natural History Society – information on the society and its activities.
http://www.benhs.org.uk

The Phasmid Study Group – a site for stick insect lovers.
http://www.stickinsect.com/

SCORECARD

The insects on this scorecard are arranged in alphabetical order. Fill in the date on which you spot an insect beside its name. A common insect scores 5 points, and a rare one is worth 25. After a day's spotting, add up all the points you've scored on a sheet of paper and keep a record of them. See if you can score more points another day.

Species (name of insect)	Score	Date spotted	Species (name of insect)	Score	Date spotted
14-spot Ladybird	15		Bombardier Beetle	15	
22-spot Ladybird	10		Brimstone	10	
Alder Fly	5		Broad-Bodied Libellula	10	
Alder Moth	20		Brown Lacewing	10	
Ant Beetle	15		Caddis Fly	10	
Ant-lion	25		Cardinal Beetle	10	
Banded Agrion	15		Carpenter Ant	25	
Bean Aphid	5		Cinnabar Moth	10	
Bee Beetle	20		Click Beetle	15	
Bee Fly	10		Clifden Nonpareil Moth	25	
Birch Sawfly	10		Clouded Yellow	15	
Black and Red Froghopper	10		Cockchafer	5	
Black and Yellow Cranefly	10		Colorado Beetle	25	
Black Ant	5		Common Cockroach	5	
Blister Beetle	25		Common Earwig	5	
Bloody-nosed Beetle	15		Common Gnat	5	
Blue Horntail	15		Common Ischnura	5	

Species (name of insect)	Score	Date spotted	Species (name of insect)	Score	Date spotted
Death Watch Beetle	25		Giant Wood Wasp	20	
Death's Head Hawk Moth	25		Glow-worm	25	
Demoiselle Agrion	15		Goat Moth	5	
Devil's Coach Horse Beetle	5		Golden-ringed Dragonfly	10	
Dor Beetle	10		Great Diving Beetle	10	
Downy Emerald	20		Great Green Bush Cricket	15	
Drone Fly	10		Great Silver Water Beetle	20	
Dung Fly	5		Green Lacewing	5	
Dusty Cockroach	15		Green Leafhopper	10	
Eared Leafhopper	20		Green Shieldbug	10	
Elephant Hawk Moth	15		Green Tiger Beetle	10	
Emperor Dragonfly	10		Green Tortoise Beetle	10	
Emperor Moth	15		Greenbottle Fly	5	
Eyed Hawk Moth	10		Grey Flesh Fly	5	
Eyed Ladybird	20		Heath Assassin Bug	10	
Fever Fly	5		Herald Moth	10	
Field Cricket	25		Holly Blue	10	
Forest Bug	10		Horned Dung Beetle	15	
Forester Moth	20		Horned Treehopper	15	
Garden Tiger Moth	5		Hornet	20	
German Cockroach	10		Horse Fly	15	
German Wasp	5		House Cricket	15	
Ghost Moth	5		Hover Fly	10	
Giant Cranefly	10		Hummingbird Hawk Moth	15	
Giant Lacewing	15		Ichneumon Wasp	10	

Species (name of insect)	Score	Date spotted	Species (name of insect)	Score	Date spotted
Lappet Moth	15		Pond Skater	5	
Large Green Ground Beetle	20		Poplar Hawk Moth	10	
Large Marsh Grasshopper	20		Potter Wasp	15	
Leaf-cutter Bee	15		Praying Mantis	25	
Lesser Earwig	15		Privet Hawk Moth	15	
Lesser Glow-worm	25		Purple Hairstreak	15	
Lesser Water Boatman	5		Puss Moth	10	
Lime Hawk Moth	10		Red and Black Burying Beetle	10	
Lobster Moth	15		Red Ant	10	
Marbled White	15		Red Underwing Moth	15	
Mayfly	10		Red-tailed Bumblebee	5	
Merveille-du-Jour Moth	15		Robber Fly	15	
Mole Cricket	25		Rose Aphid,	5	
Mother Shipton Moth	10		Rose Chafer	15	
Musk Beetle	15		Rove Beetle	5	
New Forest Cicada	25		Ruby-tailed Wasp	10	
Nut Weevil	5		Ruddy Darter	10	
Oak Apple (or gall) Gall-wasp	5		Sand Wasp	10	
Oak Eggar Moth	15		Saucer Bug	10	
Oak Marble (or gall) Gall-wasp	5		Scarlet-tipped Flower Beetle	10	
Oil Beetle	15		Scorpion Fly	10	
Peach Blossom Moth	10		Seven-spot Ladybird	5	
Peacock	5		Silver Y Moth	5	
Pearl-bordered Fritillary	20		Six-spot Burnet Moth	10	
Pied Shieldbug	10		Snake Fly	15	

Species (name of insect)	Score	Date spotted	Species (name of insect)	Score	Date spotted
Southern Cicada	25		Wasp Beetle	10	
Speckled Bush Cricket	10		Water Beetle	10	
Stag Beetle	20		Water Boatman	10	
Stick Insect	25		Water Cricket	20	
Stonefly	10		Water Measurer	10	
Swallow-tailed Moth	10		Water Scorpion	10	
Tree Wasp	10		Water Stick Insect	15	
Two-spot Ladybird	5		Whirligig Beetle	5	
Vapourer Moth	5		Wood Ant	10	
Velvet Ant	15		Wood Cricket	15	
Violet Ground Beetle	5		Wood Tiger Moth	15	
Wall Brown	10		Yellow Meadow Ant	5	
Wart-biter	25		Yellow-tail Moth	5	

NOTES

INDEX

"No of course not. I admit I was totally in the wrong. He just looked so nice and his smile is just like Elizabeth's –" She saw Hannah's expression and stopped short. "It won't happen again. I promise."

"No it won't. Anyway I've kept you long enough. I'll see you tomorrow."

Janet looked relieved.

"And take the flowers with you. Give them to your mother."